JOHN'S
STORY

COPYRIGHT

Published in paperback, 2023, in association with:
JV Author Services
www.jvauthorservices.co.uk
jvpublishing@yahoo.com

ISBN: 9798856094106

DEDICATION

To my wife, Val, for her support and love.

ACKNOWLEDGEMENTS

Thanks to Vicky and John from JV Author Services for allowing me to tell my story.

INTRODUCTION

Physically abused and strenuously worked as a small child, John endured the kind of treatment that would, at one time, have been found in the pages of a Charles Dickens story set in a workhouse.

John's account can be very harrowing and unimaginable. Reading on, you will sense the insecurity that he experienced as a small child. His parents, who he should have been able to turn to, were the very ones that dished out the cruelty.

If this had been in England's Victorian era, John would not have been alone in his suffering, as so many children were abused and used for slave labour.

But this is not the Victorian era.

He is a doting father to his two daughters, Kylie and Laura, and a devoted husband to his wife, Valerie. John feels now is the right time to relate his experiences, feelings and emotions.

This is John's life.

EARLY DAYS

I was born on the 27th of July 1939 in Teigh – that's Ruckland. Born the second eldest, I had four sisters when we lived there.

We moved to Ashwell and then on to Harlaxton. I was christened in Harlaxton by a German vicar. We didn't know that he was German at the time. At night when the German planes used to fly over, he would put a torch under a white sheet. On the top of the sheet was a swastika, and the torch beam pointed towards Coventry. He was shining the way to Coventry and ensuring he wasn't bombed. Some vicar! He was reported in the end.

This is my story from four years old. From this young age, I started my working life, but not in the traditional sense of the word. Every day, I would collect water from the pump located in the village. As you can imagine, this was a considerable task for someone so young. From this tender age, my life did not get any easier, and the chores increased as I got older.

My relationship with my father was poor, and he was a difficult man to get along with. There was a rumour within the family that he had been dropped on his head at birth which may have contributed to his temperament.

My father was in the home guard, and he used to walk around the village at night with a 303 rifle but no bullets. Perhaps that was just as well, knowing the temper he had.

One of the stories I remember about my father was the day the vicar asked him, "Could you please help free a dog from under a grave in the graveyard?"

My father went straight to the graveyard and dug down. The dog was stuck under the coffin, which was a sad sight.

The grave on the left where Father broke into the coffin

My father gave the box an almighty bang with the spade, and the coffin fell to bits. He grabbed the dog by its back legs and pulled it out. It was a spaniel – a beautiful black and white one. Would you believe the dog had dug to the bottom of the hole looking for rabbits?

Digging the grave to find the dog was illegal. My father had no right to smash a grave open like that. It was totally thoughtless. After he freed the dog from the hole, he filled it all back in, and he thought the whole situation was funny.

The house I lived in as a boy

A lady who lived two doors away from us liked me a lot. I was always around there. She was so nice. She wanted to adopt me, but Mother would not have any of it. A little while after, she took her own life. She put a pipe from the exhaust into the car, and the fumes killed her.

While we were living at Harlaxton, the 'Yanks' were always calling. They would leave sweets and tins of meat for Mum.

We witnessed a lot of German activity. At night their planes would fly over our house, and Mum would call out, "Get under the stairs. Gerry's coming." Sometimes we would watch them fly over, and Mum would say, "They're going to bomb Coventry."

On the road to Grantham one day, a German plane flew over our heads. It was so low we could see the pilot, and behind him was a Spitfire firing at 'Gerry'. There was a big bang, and he went up in smoke. My sister was in the pram, and I stood holding the handles with Mother. We watched the lot. It didn't seem to bother Mother, but 'Gerry' could have opened fire. We could have been killed when you think about it. The German planes used to fly to Grantham Town to bomb. They were after the ammunition factory called 'Moco'. They never hit the place, and it still stands today.

The pump I carried water from whatever the weather

We moved on to Manthorpe Village, where life became a 'slight' Hell, as you would say. The house in Manthorpe Village had no electricity and no running water, so I had to fetch the water from the pump in the village. Summertime was not too bad, but the winter was sheer hell. The water would spill down my legs and into my shoes until they were wet through, and ice used to form on my socks. Opposite the pump was a bus stop. I could see people laughing at me as I slipped and slid about. It was all right for them, they had running water. I got used to the 'pee taking', though. Mrs Christopher lived one to the right, opposite the water pump. She was a lovely lady. During the winter, when the water pump was frozen over, she placed hot water in a pan on top of the frozen water, and that was nearly every day.

JOBS TO DO

Along with my job of collecting water every day, I would shop for groceries – which was a mile and a half to the shop and the same back. On a Monday, the worst day of the week, I had to fill the copper and loads of buckets with water from the pump.

Entrance to the farm where I collected milk daily

I would light the copper fire, then stack all the logs at the side. When this was done, I went down to the farm and fetched the milk.

After returning from the shop, I was expected to fill a cart with wood, bring it home and saw it up. I then made my way to school – another mile and a half each way – in all weathers. My shoes leaked, and I put cardboard inside them to absorb the water. As you can imagine, this wasn't very nice when it rained heavily or snowed.

As a young boy, I spent long hours turning fresh peas in the hot, boiling sun. Not once as a child did I ever get paid for doing all the errands and jobs I used to do. If anything, it felt like a full-time job. As a child, not only did I turn the peas, but I picked them too. I also did this with my school. I went to work in a pult hole, which was a very dusty job. It was another one I never got paid for, but then again, even if I had, I wouldn't have seen the money as my father used to keep it for himself.

I didn't have a good childhood. I worked all my young life and never had a chance to enjoy myself like the other kids down my street.

My nerves were so bad as a child that I regularly wet the mattress I slept on, and the fleas within it used to bite my neck. These sorts of things would not be acceptable nowadays. People would be put away for being so cruel to a child.

My school days were not much better. I used to take bread and jam to school for dinner wrapped up in a newspaper in my pocket because we couldn't afford any school dinners. I had to sit in the shelter in the park to eat it. One day a teacher saw me in the park and, after that, insisted I sit with the other children who could afford meals. It was so embarrassing. They used to take the 'pee' and say, "Poor little boy can't afford dinner." It was not very enjoyable, and I couldn't wait to leave school.

The school had the Harvest Festival, and we all had to take something in, but I didn't have anything to give. We had the service, and then they let us go home. On the way home, I was eating an apple, and one of the boys told a teacher I had stolen it from church – a lie. I may have been poor, but I was never a thief. The next day, I was taken around the classes and caned in front of the children for something I hadn't done. The bastard wouldn't believe me. He didn't give a damn. My hands were blue for something I hadn't done. A good day? I don't think so.

As you can tell, I didn't enjoy school very much. I didn't seem to get much help from the teachers, and it seemed the best pastime for the other boys in school was to bully me. The teachers would look but didn't seem to care about it at all. That was how it was then.

I was pushed off a wall and cut my tongue, but they didn't take me to the hospital like they would these days. It was bleeding all day and very sore. When I got home, Mother took me to Dr Gibbs, and he stitched my tongue up for me. The school could have done something about it, but they would rather give you the cane as soon as look at you. Some of the teachers thought they were God.

When we got home from the doctor, I couldn't eat for a while. After my little accident, life returned to normal – regular chores, fetching, and carrying for everyone.

Naturally, I started to rebel with all the things that used to happen to me. I skipped school for six weeks when I was about eleven years old and spent the days watching the trains. I saw the Flying Scotsman, the Mallard, and the Bluebird go by, and the train drivers would give you a little wave as they passed. When it was about half past three, I would make my way home. I didn't tell anyone what I was up to. It was lonely, and the days were long. When it rained, it was miserable, and I would shelter under the railway tunnel. It was fine for a while, and I didn't harm anyone else, but when they found out what I'd been doing, all hell was let loose. The moral of this story – DON'T GET CAUGHT!

As the trains went by, the coal vibrated on the tenders of the train, but it was not wasted as I used to pick up the bits of coal off the railway line and take them home with me. Sometimes the bits were huge, but they would all come in handy to put on the fire and keep our living room warm.

WINTER

Winter came, and the nights grew dark. The fire was in the middle of the room, but it used to get very cold there in the winter. We had an old wooden chair near the door that led upstairs. It was filthy indeed.

One night at about seven o'clock, Father peeled some onions and fried them. He sat there dipping his bread into the fat and had the lot to himself. He had my sisters near him, sitting in the warm spots, but I was in the good old draught. It was nice to be loved.

Father came down with the flu and had to stop in bed for two weeks. So, as usual, I had to get on with the chores after school.

All we got was him shouting down, "Keep bloody quiet."

I wasn't allowed to talk, let alone have the radio on, miserable git! I couldn't wait for him to get better.

When Father was ill, Mr Leadham came and shouted up the stairs, "Alright?"

"Ya!" he replied.

"Get well soon. Want you back as soon as possible," he said.

"OK."

The sooner, the better, I thought. He was a miserable bastard when he was ill – even more unbearable. I was glad to see the back of him when he went to work. The money wasn't good, but you got eggs, potatoes, swedes, rabbits, apples out of the orchard, plums, and gooseberries, and we'd get our milk. On some occasions, when they killed a pig, you got lucky for some bacon. Oh yes, very good. Mind you, they would expect you to work for sweet F.A. Tight as ducks' arses, and that's putting it mildly.

With winter approaching, they wanted potato pickers. I put my hand up for this. At least I'd get paid for it, which was a bit of luck. The lorry picked me up every day for two weeks, and they paid me £2.50 (£2.10 shillings.)

My mates could buy fags and suchlike with their money. Unfortunately, I had to hand it all over. I hoped things would improve when I left school to go to Huntingtower.

Mr Priest offered me a paper round – two shillings a week. Mr Swallow had a bike in his yard and wanted ten shillings for it. He said I could pay him two shillings a week, and then I could have it. That was great. I soon paid for it and could ride the long journey to school. Mr Swallow was one of the good men in the village.

SCHOOL

The days passed slowly until I could leave school (a horrible place.) One day we had to go swimming, so we set off for the baths, and the teacher asked me, "Where are your trunks?"

I told him I didn't have any because Mother couldn't afford them, so the teacher set off to the office to get me some. I was looking forward to this as it was a treat to go swimming. When I was changing into them, he saw the bruises and blue marks across my legs and bottom and asked, "How the hell did you get them?" I told him I'd fallen over. He just looked at me and then walked off. I was too scared to tell him the truth and thought he wouldn't have believed me anyway. He didn't believe me about the apple, so why bother? If Father had found out I had told on him, I would have got a lot worse – some more kicking and the belt etc. It wasn't worth telling anyone about it. Suffer in silence – the best way. I looked forward to when it would come to an end.

We had an outside toilet. On Sundays, I had to dig a hole and empty the toilet into it. I would use a long-handled ladle, and people walking past would hold their noses. God, it stank!

We had a pig in the sty, he lived off house waste, but the time had come to kill the pig. Mr Bassely came along to do this. He brought the pig out of the sty, put a rifle to its head, and the pig fell to the floor. You had to put the dead pig on a wooden rack, tip hot water over it, and scrape the hairs off it. Then it was cut open, and everything was placed in the bath. Later that day, Mr Bassely would return, cut the pig up, and put it in salt. It would stay like that for about six weeks. They would put it on the living room wall and cut it as needed. Boiled bacon! On the living room wall! It makes a change from having a picture up there.

It was almost time for me to leave school. Life was easier now that I had my bike and would soon be off to Huntingtower.

The headmaster at school was nice and asked me to look after the school chickens because of my background. I would see to them at break time, collect the eggs, and take them to his office. I had to go down and fetch the pellets from one of the shops, which was nice if the weather was good but not so if it was raining. I got out of class for a while doing this, and one teacher didn't like me leaving to do it. The teachers in the school were not all bad, I suppose. Only one pig of a teacher took pleasure in banging me about for no reason. He didn't like me at all. I just think he liked to see people crying, but he didn't make me cry. I wouldn't let him. He had several goes at it when he hit me around the head, but I've had worse, so the likes of him didn't bother me. He took us for cane work, marking trays and baskets, which was good fun, apart from him. You always have one wherever you go, and I couldn't wait to see the back of him.

The rest of the staff were good. I used to go up on the stage to read from the bible to the whole school every day. Once I got used to this, I enjoyed it, and I couldn't have been bad, or they wouldn't have had me up there to do it.

It was nearly summer – six weeks' holiday. Holiday! That's a laugh. Not for me out collecting wood and working in the fields. The barrow I collected the wood with had two big handles, two motorbike wheels, two doors on each end and a door on the bottom, and it weighed a ton. I had to go to the park to collect the wood. Going there was all right, but coming back was sheer hell. It was so heavy, and the wheels were flat, making it worse. No one would let me borrow a pump for the tyres. I think they enjoyed seeing me struggle and sniggered as they went by. Six weeks soon passed, and then it was back to school. I didn't mind it now so much because I had the bike.

When the winter months approached, it was sugar beet time – knocking and topping sugar beet before school. Apart from the sugar beet, I still had to go to the pump for water for the copper and fetch the milk. My hands were white and wrinkled with the wetness. It was 6.30 am, and I had to do this until 8.00 am. After my chores, I set out on my bike to school. Good old days, they say, I should coco! School started at 8.30 am. It was a tight ship.

HOME LIFE

Once my sister came home from service – she lived with Mrs Stevens at Harlaxton Road in Grantham. My sister borrowed Mrs Stevens' pen and lost it in our house. I was accused of stealing it, and she was going to call the police, but she found it. She was a right old cow that Mrs Stevens. I told Mother that I had not seen the pen, but no one seemed to take any notice.

One day, when I was hungry, I got out the cake, pulled the wrapper down, and dug the middle out with a spoon. I took the whole of the inside out.

Then, when Father came home from work, he asked Mother, "Do you want some cake?" He'd cut into it, and this time it caved in. He said, "Wait until I see Arthur on Saturday. I'm gonna tell 'im where to get off!"

If he had known it was me, he would have killed me.

One time near Christmas, we were putting the Christmas tree up with Mars bars hung on it. I felt a bit peckish, so I took the Mars bar out of its wrapper and stuck the ends up so nobody would notice. After a few days, he says, "I'll have a Mars, Mother." When he grabbed hold of it, it was empty. He went mad but never found out it was me, thank Christ.

The Chestnut tree where we plucked the birds

As kids, we had to pluck poultry, ducks, geese, chickens, pheasants, and partridges. We'd sit under the chestnut tree in all weathers. Rabbits had to be gutted for the people in the village, year in, year out until I left school. I didn't get paid for it.

One night I was sent to the vicarage with some prepared geese on a willow pattern plate. Just as I got to the church gate, something frightened me, and I dropped the plate and ran home. I was promptly sent back to pick them all up, wash them all, and then return to the vicarage with them. I got in a lot of trouble.

I could tell when summer was on its way – long hours, dawn to dusk, in the fields turning peas and stacking wheat and barley. All the other kids in the village played cricket and football. I just carried on working in the fields. When I got home after putting the hours in, the first thing would be, "Go to the pump for water." On a recent visit to the village, I saw that the old water pump was still there. Seeing it gave me mixed feelings, but it certainly can't be looked at as an old friend. Water pump! Nothing changes.

After a day's work in the fields, I looked forward to supper and then off to bed to be up early and slog on again. Mother was also out working, but she was only helping out so they could get the harvest in quicker.

On one particular occasion, I had just got home from the fields, and Mother told me to go and get the girls in. They were playing in the field behind the house. I was walking across to get them, and one of the boys was chasing them around the barley stack with a pitchfork. As he came running around the stack, he drove both the tines through both my legs up to the kneecaps. Everyone ran away, including my sisters, and left me on my own with both tines through my leg. I pulled the fork out myself, and the blood poured down my legs. When I eventually managed to walk home, Mother sent me down to the village nurse, and she took me to hospital. We had to walk there, that is. I got them fixed up and had to walk back home again. It was back to normal the next day. You've guessed it. "Go to the pump for water!"

My sisters never seemed to care, and it was through them that I got the pitchfork injury. The girls seemed to get away with murder in our household. I only had to step a little out of line and get the belt and boot.

At night I had a treat. We used to listen to 'Dick

Barton' on the radio. I'd sit down, listen and look at my hands that were red raw. The radio had an accumulator, and the batteries had to be charged weekly. One set had to go on charge down at Coomes shop. So, one of my other chores was to pick it up on the way home from school. It was so heavy, but it wasn't half as heavy as the coal I had to carry from the yard. If it was wet, the coal would soak right through to your clothing, and I would carry it on my back and rest it on a wall every so often. It was murder. I was always glad to see my house on these occasions.

Another of my chores was carrying the groceries home for Mrs Doughty and also the paraffin from Belton. I had to bring it in a five-gallon drum and walk about two miles with it. The handle would cut through my hands, but there was always a nice piece of cake at the end of this chore. Mrs Doughty was a very nice lady, and now and again, she would buy me new trousers. The poor lady had very bad asthma and could hardly breathe.

Mother was soon expecting a new baby – my brother James. Afterwards, she was so ill, so Mrs Doughty looked after me. My sisters were all farmed out to Uncle Jim at New Street in Grantham, but I had to stay home to do the fetching and carrying as usual.

People in the village also helped by cooking meals as Mother was hospitalised for quite some time. I would collect the meals (two dinners and two puddings) from different houses every day, but there was never any food for me, I just had to do the fetching. They wanted to send her to Ropsley Asylum, but Father wouldn't have any of it. He said she was coming home, and that was the end of it. He told the nurses he would look after her, but he never did. When she came home, she didn't know what day it was or what was going on.

One day, Father came by the house on the horse and cart, and Mother was boiling some stuff called a bread poultice in a grey tin. She was suffering from milk fever and had a big hole in her left breast. The tin was being boiled up on a 'Primus' stove. You started it with meths, and then you turned on the paraffin. Father came up the path like a bat out of hell, took the tin off the stove, and threw it over the wall.

He then turned on me and backhanded me, shouting, "Don't let her do that again." Why? I don't know. Probably just another excuse to lay into me. Then away he went on the cart. I had just turned my back for a second, and then, bang, she struck me over the head with her copper stick. I saw stars. How the hell it didn't kill me, I'll never know.

"Go and get that 'fooking' pot," she barked. I didn't know whether I was coming or going. I climbed over the wall but couldn't get back, so I climbed over the front gate and handed it to her – tin and poultice. She started boiling it again. When it was ready, she took the bread out, put it in my hand, and told me to hold it on her breast. It was disgusting. So bloody awful. A small child having to do this, with yellow 'goodness knows what' coming out. But my mother was so ill at the time, and I had no choice.

Mother even thought that Father was having an affair with the vicar's wife, and she went charging down the path to go and do something about it. But things managed to calm down, and it all blew over, thank goodness.

One day, while she was in this state of mind, I came home from school. I had just got in, and she came at me with the copper stick again, and boy, did she get me right over the head with it. After that, I made sure that when I was near her that she wasn't armed. With the blows rained down on my head, it's a wonder I was never seriously ill, let alone killed. I must have been made of pretty tough stuff. She would have been better off being cared for in a special hospital because she was mentally ill. She did get better, but it took a hell of a long time.

Some things you never forget. One day Mother and Father locked us in the back room and told us to keep quiet. They tied a rope from one door handle across to another. One of my sisters started to swing on the rope, and the mangle was knocked and started rocking, ready to fall over. I dived over her, and the mangle came crashing down on the table and smashed it to bits. Christ! When Father came in, all hell was let loose. I was booted, belted, and kicked. I don't know how many times, but I was beaten senseless. My sister got away with it again, and I was blamed for the lot. It didn't end there, though. I was immediately sent upstairs to my mattress – a poor excuse for a bed in the corner of the top room. Flock it was, with a bloody big hole in it. It had loads of fleas and smelled of piss, which I had to lie in. There I was for at least four days. I used to go to school smelling of 'roses', I don't think.

Teachers used to say to me, "You stink."

They could be very cruel, but I could do nothing about it, as I used to 'pee' myself so much when I was ill-treated.

During my confinement to my mattress, not once did my sisters bring drink or food. It was sheer hell. Father would come home from work, call me down, and boot and belt me. I would wet down my legs with fright, and then he would send me back up again.

Once, I had the pleasure of sleeping in the pig sty. Luxury. It had straw in there, and it was warm. The pig was not present at the time, by the way.

I sometimes wonder how I made it through boyhood. But there you go – I did. He must have been shining on me.

On the Saturday after my confinement, Father said, "We're going rabbiting." After my time upstairs, this was heaven because I knew I'd get something to eat when we got home. It'd been nearly a whole week without any food. Off we went, and my mate Alan came along as well. It wasn't long before we got a couple of rabbits. Walking along, we came to a gate. Alan and I climbed over, and then Father did, but he slipped and fell on his balls. Of course, I laughed, and so did Alan (justice at last, but justice was short-lived.)

In his temper, he got the spade and smashed me over the head with it and said, "Take that, you bastard. It will teach you to laugh!"

My head was ringing. Alan just looked at my father with complete disgust. To cap it all, after this blow, Father made me stick my head down to have a look in a rabbit hole. A rabbit appeared alright, at a rate of knots. Bang. It hit me right in the middle of the head, just after the rattle on the brains with the bloody spade. Life was so good, I don't think. This treatment comes as no surprise after the week I'd had.

SUNDAYS

Sunday was the best day of the week – roast dinner. But the pleasures are short-lived – the garden needs to be watered. What do I have to do? "Go to the pump for water." More than one trip to the pump seems endless. All Father did was sit on the wall and watch. All the other boys were having a good time being children, enjoying ice creams, and playing games – football and cricket in the village. I got sweet FA.

One Sunday, Mother was baking a cake. Father had gone fishing with one of his mates, and Mother was expecting visitors – Uncle Jim. She made him some tea in the best cups that came out on Sundays for visitors only. When Father came in, he rolled back the table cloth, filled his shaving mug with hot water, propped his shaving mirror up against the cake stand – complete with Mother's cake – and started shaving. Mother had a go at him. He turned around and shouted at her, "It's my 'fooking house!" Arrogant bastard. He had no thoughts for anyone else.

There was a man called Mr Harrison, and when we caught a lot of rabbits, he would take me to Sleaford Market. It would give me a day out – I used to enjoy that. There were some lovely people about. Mrs Daft (the lady with the wart remedy mentioned later) was very nice and used to help me a lot.

COUNTRY LIFE

Getting on to the crueller elements of life in the country – and it was cruel. I can remember as a child when they would castrate the little lambs. I thought this was barbaric, and if this was practised now, all hell would be let loose, and rightly so too. This is what they would do, believe it or not.

A man would hold the lamb on his shoulders, and they would hold the lamb's legs apart. Then, they would cut their little ball bags at the back of the lamb. A man would pull the balls with his teeth and spit them into a bowl. Beautiful memories. Then they would cut the lamb's tail off and let it go into the pen, the blood pouring from its tail and little ball bags. It was so cruel. A woman would wait until this was all done and then take the bowl, wash them and cook them to serve them up for dinner. I suppose you would say that she was eating bollocks and plenty of them. I don't know if she had them with bread or soup. I never bothered asking. It makes a change from talking bollocks!

Another incident I will never forget was when a cow was calving because the bullock hadn't been castrated properly. Sadly, the calf had died and was stuck inside her. The vet arrived and gave me instructions on how to help him. I wore a big apron and had to put a special saw around my thumbs and then place my hands inside the cow. I followed the vet's instructions and proceeded to saw the dead calf in half so that it could be removed. Once this was done, covered in blood, I felt for its feet, attached a rope, and we pulled it out. The dead calf was placed on the floor and skinned, and then the vet left, leaving me to clean myself up.

I got a job on another farm and had to cycle eight miles to get there. The calves hadn't been fed on my first day, so I sorted and cleaned them. I was expected to scythe the grass as it was not a mechanical farm. I worked here for around three or four months. The farmer didn't want me to leave but wouldn't offer me any extra money to stay.

When I was working on the farm in winter, the fields would flood and freeze. It would take a huge hammer to break up the frozen lumps of clay before it could be rotavated.

Sometimes people did not know how to communicate in those days. My mate Tony's dad used to come home from work and knock the hell out of his wife, and she was having a baby at the time. She would have a meal ready for him and had been baking cakes all day. He kicked his little boy over about six rows of spuds. A little time after this, she left him. He got a girlfriend and did exactly the same again.

ACCIDENTS

One day, Father sent me to Mrs Mountain for some turf fags, just across the road from us. I collected them, and on the way over, a car came round the corner, hit me straight up the arse, and knocked me up in the air about ten feet. The fags went everywhere, so I picked them up and put them back in their box. I got home, too scared to say anything. The driver knocked at the door a while later, and Mother answered it.

"Is your boy alright?" the driver asked. "I've just knocked him over!"

I was lucky, I suppose, that day. I was not taken to the hospital as you would be now. I had a lot of bruises on my bottom, back, and legs. It shook me up some. After that, I always made sure it was safe to cross.

Where I got the fags from, I was caught now and again by Mrs Mountain to make butter. I had to keep turning this barrel with a handle on it, with the sour milk inside. I had to keep turning and turning until it was butter. She would then weigh it into pounds and sell it. While making the butter, she would smoke like a trooper, and sometimes the ash would fall into the butter. I suppose it made it taste better. She was a tight old cow. I would do all that work, and she didn't even give me a tanner. I was cheap labour. I could just about turn the bloody handle. Her old man was a miserable git, but he had some good points. He loved his bowls and was good at it too.

One stormy day I was stacking wheat in the field. There was a terrible storm. The sky was black – as black as night. The only time you ever saw the outlines of the houses and trees was when the lightning would light up the black starry sky. The rain beat down on me, and I was soaked, cold and shivering. The water ran down my back and neck, making my hairs stand up like soldiers on parade. After a while, I stood under the stacks to shelter until it stopped. Suddenly, there was a huge bang, and lightning struck the stacks I was standing under. There was smoke, thick and black, blowing all over the place. God must have been watching over me, or else that burning wheat would have been me. I could have died under there.

I was working in the fields with Mother and the dog ran off. Mother made me chase it and when we found it, the dog had disappeared into a rabbit hole. Mother asked me to dig into the hole. I dug down seven or eight feet, grabbed the dog and lifted it out to her. The soil collapsed on top of me, but Mother just took the dog and went home. When I managed to get myself out, I went back with the rabbits I had caught and said to Mother, "I could've died back there." She didn't care, she just wanted the rabbits to sell.

Road to the farm where I worked in the fields with Mother

Another close encounter was when I was fishing using a forty-foot rod. Out of the blue, a lightning bolt struck the tree behind me. The tree came crashing down just metres away, but once again, I was lucky to survive.

SPOOKY TIMES

When I was a young boy, I saw some sights in my life, some really nasty ones. Some sights that would make your hair curl. You move on with your life, but I have never forgotten the things I saw and how it affected me.

In my house, there was a nasty, evil presence. Some would call it an evil spirit, but whatever it was, it was a nasty spirit. It used to follow my mother from the kitchen into the living room and yank and pull her hair. You never saw what the spirit looked like as it was invisible. All you saw was my mum's hair being pulled. It never affected her. You could say she was used to it. It happened regularly – too often if you ask me.

Our parson who used to live down the road came to exorcise it from the house. He tried everything but to no avail. I guess you could say the ghost wanted to stay, not just for a week but for life.

Continuing from the strange goings on in my

house, early one morning, I climbed out of my bedroom window to go fishing with my mate Chris. We went to a lake called Collotaurpe Lake. I really don't know how to explain this, but I will do my best. It was about three thirty in the morning, and it was just breaking light. A fine white mist appeared in front of Chris while we fished. Chris started speaking to this mist, and a voice said, "Goodbye, my son." Me and Chris continued to fish for the rest of the morning then I walked with Chris back to his house. His dad was outside waiting for him with a solemn look on his face and said, "Son, I have some bad news. Your mother died at three thirty this morning."

He looked up at his dad with tears in his eyes and replied, "Yes, Dad, I know. She came to see me and said goodbye to me."

It sounds weird, but it's true. As they say, strange but true.

THE VICARAGE

The photo of the vicarage below is where a man called Mr Franks used to live. He didn't buy the place – it was rented from the church, and he kept turkeys around the back of the church in a huge garden.

He didn't keep them as pets but used to kill them, and once nicely cooked, he would put them on the table for dinner. My father would help him and would hang them alive. He would tie their legs and feet up and hang them up with a nail on the wall – the feathers would flap about all over the place. He would then get a pocketknife and stick it into their necks so they would bleed to death. My father used to say he would do this as it would make the turkeys whiter.

I personally thought it was barbaric and cruel. I'm an animal lover and hated seeing this happen. We then had to pluck them under a massive tree in the garden. My father used to look like a butcher when sticking the knives into the turkeys' necks. You would never have believed he was a father of five kids and married. Seeing the turkeys killed that way was cruel and evil, but I didn't say anything. I thought it was best to keep quiet. I did that for most of my childhood – look and listen but never speak or answer back. When my father had done the deed for Mr Franks, the vicar would give him a thank you present of Young's Beer. Sometimes a few bottles, and if he was in a good mood, it would be a crate.

I remember the weekends. My father would sit on the wall with a white bowl in his hand, catching the blood as it dropped into the bowl.

I went to the pump to get water for the flowers in the front garden – a gorgeous row of sweet peas. These were his pride and joy. I had to put the stirrup pump into the bucket, and my father held the hose and watered the front garden. I stopped to catch my breath, and then I refilled my bucket again and again. Although I couldn't complain as it was a sunny day.

GOOD OLD DAYS

You know what? Life was great. In those days, you didn't have taps or a proper toilet. If you did, it was not indoors. It was right down the end of the garden. If you didn't know any better, you would have thought it was a shed, not to mention that there was no power, just candles. The radios were battery-powered, and we didn't have electric fires.

It was all about having coal and logs on the fire to keep our home heated and warm, and when winter came, my God, did you freeze. Sometimes you could not feel your toes or hands. They were numb from the cold.

When my sister left to get married, I moved downstairs to the back room. I did not like my room very much. I felt like I was never alone, and there was a presence in that room. It used to breathe on the back of my neck every night and make the hairs stand up. It would open my bedroom door, and although I was used to it, it was not pleasant in the slightest. It would then leave my room and go into my sisters'. They used to yell and scream, but my father never got out of bed to see if his daughters were OK. Instead, he shouted from his bedroom, "Shut up and go back to sleep."

He was never bothered about us. All he cared about was himself. He could not have cared less.

End house where Sister lived

I used to pull the blanket over my head to block out my sisters' screams and the heavy breathing on my neck. Whatever it was that scared me and my sisters was very noisy. All this is so strange but very true.

THE WATCH

When my father died, Val and I went to the house in Belton Lane. It was as if we should not have been there. No one welcomed us, and you could cut the air with a knife. When the hearse came, Val and I followed it to the crematorium, parked up, and went to the front of the church. The funeral seemed to go on forever. The church was full, but there were only five wreaths. That's all he had – you could see he was very popular.

After the funeral, we went to a hall at the back of Mother's for tea and cakes. What a waste of time that was going back there. We were not made welcome at all. They made you feel like a bastard at a family reunion.

This brought to mind when I was six years old, my uncle had a watch, and he said he would leave it to me. After Dad had died, and after the funeral, I asked Mother for it.

"I don't know where it is, boy!" she replied.

My sister Evelyn did, though.

She phoned me at home and said, "I will hand it over to you when you come down next."

This was a while after the funeral, and when we were there, and I asked her about it again, she denied all knowledge of it.

This happened in front of Mother, and she said, "I don't know where it is. If I did, you could have it."

My sister just sat there. I had no idea at the time, but both my little girls heard her say – maybe this was during the phone call she made to me – it's in the top drawer in the bedroom. She got up suddenly, and by some strange miracle, she went and found it, and she was supposed to be family.

This promised watch was finally mine. Uncle Jim died nine years ago, so obviously, no one was in a hurry for me to obtain my keepsake – my memory of Uncle Jim. It just shows their mentality, treating me as a black sheep, and I always will be.

While I was at the funeral, my brother's girlfriend came up and asked me in a very 'tactful' way, "You're the one with THAT disease, MS?"

I said, "No. You've got that wrong. It's Multifocal Motor Neuropathy with induction block!" That stopped her in her tracks. I thought, "Pick the bones out of that, you b-------!"

Multifocal Motor Neuropathy with induction block were the only words I said all bloody day! My brother didn't have two words to say to me, and if I had spoken my mind to any of them, I would definitely not have been Mr Popular. The truth always gets to people if the cap fits.

I do have to say, there were some decent beings at

the funeral – the only ones who showed any compassion for myself and Val – Lionel's daughters. They were very nice. My mother's sister's boys, and Uncle George's wife. Uncle George was Mother's brother, and he is gone now. Rhoda – she was another nice one – my mother's sister, the youngest. She had not long lost her husband. She used to live with us when I was a little boy. She was with us for quite some time and could tell a tale or two about the family.

She worked at a farm across the way. It was a farm with goats, chickens, plough land, and a big orchard with pears and apples. One night, poor Rhoda was sitting on the pig manure heap reading a paper, and HE threw a bucket of water all over her. A bucket of water I had to fetch, of course! She was not too pleased, I can tell you. But she still laughed at it. They were hard days for her too. She met and married Alan, who died two weeks before my father.

If the events contained in these pages were to happen in this day and age, people, next-door neighbours and their friends, the decent people of this society, would soon act if it were brought to their attention. Social Services, the police and Childline would be there. It's such a shame it's taken this long. Forgive me for sounding off so, but the harsh memories of my childhood bring nothing but pain. It's a bitter pill to swallow. Thank God that pain and suffering can be stopped for helpless children these days, and also, children know their rights. Which is not a bad thing, provided they don't push things too far with their parents.

As a young lad, I had no one to go to, and no one wanted to know anyway.

If someone did buy me something, maybe

something little, whatever, it meant so much. Just that act of kindness went a long way.

Life got a lot better for me when I left the village. I have not looked back since – that's for sure.

TIPS AND TRICKS

The following are some of the things I have learned or heard over the years from different people.

A good bait for catching fish: you need oil of Rapeseed, oil of Aniseed, and oil of Juniper. Mix it with pig meal, chopped worms and a pint of pig's blood that had gone dry. This mix used to stink to high heaven, but it was a hell of a good Tench bait. Then just use worms only. The water in front of you used to boil with fish, and then when it got warm, they would be on the top. If people were walking by, they would hold their noses because of the smell. This is not an anglers tale. They did this. We had drums of blood in the backyard, and as soon as it was dry, we'd mix it as bait. As you took the lid off the drum, the stink was awful. But when they stopped the home killing of pigs, this practice also died a death.

Old boys and old sayings. Here's one:

"Have seen the whistling wolf full nests and the Osoling bird too."

Crazy people but humorous at times. They would also come out with, "Go to the shop for a pint of pigeons milk."

Or, "Go to the shop for a left-handed spanner."

"Lost a bob and found a tanner."

AND, "He got the pip and cart squeak."

STRANGE BUT TRUE!

When I was about six, I had warts on my hands and arms. A lady named Mrs Daft mixed up some sulphur and lard, applied it and wrapped them in bandages. All the warts disappeared. Good old remedies that worked.

This one's a winner. Listen to this one.

An old chap in the village used to say, "Grab a toad and kill it, and bury it in a red ant hill for six weeks. Go back after this time and grab all the bones, then throw them in a stream. The bone that goes upstream, you have to run like mad to catch it. If you succeed in this, then go out at midnight, and you'll meet the Devil!"

Strange people in this village, yes? It must be the water.

All you hay fever sufferers out there, this remedy is for you, and it works. This one came from an old lady in the village. First thing in the morning, give your nose a good old blow and then put some Vaseline up each nostril. Vaseline traps the pollen. Pollen gets worse as the day goes on, and this should ease your suffering. Also, for a bad cold, one tablespoon of honey, one of vinegar, and one of butter. Melt it in the oven, stir it around, and then down the hatch. Hey presto, go to bed, and in the morning, you are OK after the sweat you lost.

TO LIGHTEN THE MOOD

It was Christmas day in the workhouse,
The snow was raining fast,
And a barefooted girl with shoes on
Stood sitting in the grass

(This was a quote from an old boy in the village who
was always telling me tales.)

EPILOGUE

Although my story is hard to read at times, it is a true account of what happened to me in my childhood. Thankfully, I have gone on to have many happy memories, but I can never forget my upbringing and the scars it left me with.

Printed in Great Britain
by Amazon